Higher Than You Can Soar

Shbrone Mims
Illustration by Gwendolyn Davis

Outskirts Press, Inc.

Denver, Colorado

Outskirts Press, Inc.
http://www.outskirtspress.com

ISBN: 978-1-4327-1838-1

Outskirts Press and the "OP" logo are trademarks belonging to Outskirts Press, Inc.

PRINTED IN THE UNITED STATES OF AMERICA

It's been five years since I have seen him. It's been five years since his quest to make the impossible – possible. But to think of all the good times we shared, my mind would need to ponder a bit further in the past.

Back in time we knew as our first spring. Back in time when our mothers hatched us to the world we knew nothing of, and fed us beak to beak. Back to when our fathers acted as protectors of their flock, and were hunters – not the hunted. Even further back, when snowcapped mountains, luscious green rainforests, pristine lakes and streams were not threatened; but flourished immensely to the naked eye. Oh yes, I see it now, I thought the years past would've clouded those memories forever. It was when seasons' changes meant winter, spring, summer and fall. And daffodils, honeysuckles and apple blossoms awake yearly from their hiatus; while caterpillars, hummingbirds and honeybees eagerly welcomed their return.

It was the first time we laid eyes on one another as we took our first flight, but couldn't finish our expected journey, because we couldn't take our eyes from the beauty we saw in each other.

That's how it began, the two of us crash landing in a thicket of brush, because instead of looking forward we chose to look backward at each other, as if we were in a hypnotic trance. It was the first of many wonderful – yet unusual days of our lives. It was the first time we met, five years ago.

I am told, long since day was considered a beginning and night an ending, birds of migration have flocked south for the winter and returned north for the spring. This was something not questioned because there were no questions about it. Something within us, a biological clock some called it, told us it's time to migrate. And if by chance we were steered off course during our flight; it acted as a compass guiding us accurately to our winter retreat. A unique possession one would think, but it's often envied by those who don't understand its function.

But just three years before our time – mine and Randall's, this unique possession was threatened. And since our time that margin has narrowed. Something was wrong we were told, and it was not our doing, we were constantly reminded. A wiser animal was to blame, and he cared nothing about correcting the problem because maybe he's the one who envied us most, we were constantly shown.

It seemed like everyday our lives consisted of nothing but stories of our demise. And perhaps that's why Randall and I did what we did every chance we got – which usually was every day – take to flight just the two of us, traveling miles and miles, and leaving what we felt was out of our hands behind to those who cared to listen to such woes. We would fly as fast as we could and as far as we could, and not contemplate any return. We were kids and we vowed the burdens of the world shan't rest on our wings. We should have fun and let those before us worry about such things, so we thought. Our time is now and the many tomorrows to come; you only get one chance to be young, so take full advantage of it, and don't let it pass you by, we told each other everyday.

But one day while resting in our favorite place, where the meadow is lusciously thick and green, and the water is cool and fresh; we noticed a wolf making an approach to drink from the stream. As he did however, Randall began to notice things about him, and began to speak of them.

"Look at him," he said. "Look at the way he walks, the way he laps his water, the way he gazes into the sunset. He does everything as if it's his last time doing so."

I don't know why Randall made such observations, but he did, and when he did, the wolf lifted his head and spoke. "My hearing is keen. I hear well what you say. I wait for death everyday. What else is there for me? But if it happens, don't be sad for me. I will not be. Because being the last of my kind is a burden I have carried for many years, and my time to rest is something I welcome with my last breath." He said no more, lowered his head and resumed drinking from the clear stream. And from that day forward we realized that our many tomorrows are today, and those burdens we left so far behind had never left us; they were with us wherever we're to go, and perhaps we needed to lend our wings to lighten the load of others.

That notion Randall took more serious than I, especially when we talked to O. B. (Old Bird). He was an owl who perched in a sycamore tree a few feet from our roost. He was well respected by many because of his wisdom and age. The things he told us and showed us really got Randall concerned, in fact, so concerned I feared for his sanity. For instance, once we spent almost the entire day with him listening to his wisdom about the world and beyond. I tell you that was the day of days, and if we learned no more that's all right with me. Because what we consumed, could last us a lifetime.

He began lecturing on man, the superior animal, who in most cases was the cause of extinction of several animal groups. Be it a need for clothing, food, building expansion, pollution, or the sheer pleasure of shooting a defenseless animal, something they call a sport; we were expendable.

"We are expendable!" Randall shouted, interrupting as he did. "Don't we have a say about our lives and the world we live in?"

"If we did, young Randall, we would not be having this conversation." O. B. wisely replied. But as he did, Randall's eyes became raging red, which caused tears to stream down in disgust and disbelief.

"If this is so, why is it so?" Randall barely uttered the words between his sobbing and sniffling. "Will you please tell me why?"

"The answer you seek is up there, ***higher than you can soar***, young Randall," he said, as he pointed beyond the top of the trees – beyond the clouds and the stars. "There is one who sits there and watches all, so I am told by those before me."

He always spoke like that, metaphorically. He said in doing so, causes one to think more sincerely about what is said; and I guess it's so, because Randall and I did not immediately reply to his response. We just kept silent – replaying what was said in our thoughts, hoping to grasp its meaning. It was difficult to understand at first, but once O. B. took us a couple of other places to make his point, its meaning gradually became a bit clearer.

Our first stop was a place the humans call a zoo. There, we saw animals locked behind cages; and we quickly became saddened because their freedom was so limited – if you call what we saw freedom.

But when we landed and began to speak to them, we were surprised at some of their responses, particularly those who expressed happiness in being locked in a cage. Because they ate three meals a day, were bathed by humans, were given medicine for their health, they were content with their surroundings, as long as those meager privileges were granted.

But those were the fools, the ones who lost their savory taste of freedom. The taste that once coated their palate from sun up to sun down; so we were told by a lion that roared in pain and despair. "Idiots! Imbeciles! Are those who express such contentedness. No longer do they bare lost minds, but lost souls as well. I remember when I stalked the wilds of Africa, there I was happy. To survive, I did what

4

5

I had to do and I was respected.   Here, I survive by doing what I am told to do. There is no respect in that. Here, I am just an animal in a cage, but out there in the wilds of Africa, I was King of the Jungle." He said with a gleam in his eyes." And to accept anything less would make me what I despise most," he exclaimed, as he looked in anger at those who expressed contentedness.

Soon, we left them behind because O. B. said we had two more stops and the time was growing short. Our next landing was in front of a building that spelled the name taxidermy. There we could not believe our eyes or our hearts, because to this day, we both would swear our hearts stopped beating for a minute once we peaked inside.

"Now, those animals we left behind in the zoo – some of them had legitimate gripes and some of them did not. But, at least they had the right to express their own opinions," O. B. said. "But if you look through this window, you'll see that these animals did not have that right. Someone else expressed their opinions for them. And if you look even closer, you'll see that their expressions were definitely not theirs, yet, those expressions would remain until time has no more meaning."

We looked closely as O. B. instructed and surely enough their eyes told what they truly felt. Something, if you are human, you would never see. But, if you were an animal, you would leave knowing that is not the way you would want to spend eternity – captured in a photographic pose. I mean, after all, a camera would have done the trick!

Well, with two quick flaps of our wings, once again we found ourselves in flight with heavy thoughts in our minds, and aching hearts pounding slowly in our chests. O. B. told us we had just one more place to visit to make the journey complete. Huh, had it been left to me or Randall our journey would have ended miles ago. But as it was, he was the teacher and we were the students, and the bell had not yet toll for class dismissal.

This last place was called a circus, and there the animals were performing and doing tricks. The humans were clapping and screaming with joy – I mean the animals really made the humans happy, and the humans made them – the animals – happy. And believe it or not, we were happy also. We could not believe how our once saddened hearts were now filled with a joy that gushed rampantly to the tips of our wings and to the bottom of our feet. It was a warming sensation of inner peace and gratification that covered our bodies. A feeling our bodies longed for desperately. Because I swear – I swear, had we seen anything more depressing than what we saw earlier, O. B. would've made the trip back by himself, because Randall and I would've died on the spot.

"Do you know why I brought you here?" O. B. asked as we laughed in amusement while witnessing the many talents both the humans and animals displayed.

"No we do not," both Randall and I replied.

"As you can see, as you look in the faces of the young and the old humans, you know that those humans are indeed animal lovers. You see young Randall and Cindy, all humans aren't bad humans," O. B. explained. And when he said that, both Randall and I had to agree. Then he mentioned it was time to leave, but Randall and I had to disagree. As far as we were concerned, school was still in session, because the last act had yet to come.

Now of course those stories of the zoo, the taxidermy and the circus have been told many times before and handed down generation after generation, much like the old fable of *the tortes and the hare*. But to actually witness what's been told, well let's just say we returned home a little wiser, a little more compassionate, and had more understanding of humans than before, well so I thought. Because Randall – well, he proved me wrong. Later that day, I saw him sitting there in the meadow where humans take to flight and land – in some silly thing called an airplane. Well that's what O. B.

calls them; and the more they took off, the angrier Randall became. He had been out there a long time, I thought we were both happier now, and both understood the order of things. And could live with the humans, be it good or bad, especially if we could stay clear of the bad. But the anger in his voice, and the tears in his eyes, let me know quickly that all of that had come to pass.

I remember telling my best friend Loretta, or LoLo she's commonly called, about the whole experience. She is one I share everything with. We've been close since we were chicks barely out the nest. We confided our deepest emotions with one another; and that particular day was no different. But while I was trying to express my concerns for Randall's uncontrollable rage toward the humans, she was trying to convince me about her boyfriend Bryan being the best thing to ever happen to her. Ya see, I didn't like old baldy – well that's what I called him. He was a bald eagle, not a bird of migration like me and LoLo, one who thought he was every female's wildest dream, with his stunning plum of feathers, his big protruding muscles, and large wing span that stretched to eternity. Why shoot! The humans marveled at his larger than life soaring prowess. Huh now, look at me carrying on like LoLo about this conceited clown – but shoot they did. They even put him and his kind on something called money, and placed them on a piece of cloth called a flag in some parts of the world. And if that wasn't enough, they protected his kind from being hunted – no wonder his head was so swollen with arrogance. I tell ya, I can't stand him, particularly when he flexes his chiseled body and says stupid stuff like: "We eagles don't have to migrate south for the winter, because we are well suited for whatever nature has to offer." Yeah he said that alright, with that silly wide grin of his.

And poor LoLo, he's got her head in a tail spin. She couldn't even think straight when she's gracing his presence. She told me not to worry about Randall, he always becomes angry when he doesn't understand things. Just like the time we first met another friend of ours named Curtis the worm, ahh I mean the caterpillar, he'll kill me for calling him a worm.

We wouldn't let Randall eat him because we learned he was an orphan, and the last of his kind. He was left behind by his family, because for some strange reason he didn't receive his wings. But this didn't matter to Randall any, as far as he was concerned, a worm was dinner to any bird. So he cussed us good, and even wanted to fight for that delicacy. But we eventually calmed him down when we told him to walk in Curtis' shoes and see how that feels. So from that day forward, we would always see after Curtis, making sure he had plenty to eat, a warm place to lay his head, and we'd spread the word to other birds that he's a rare species, and if eaten, his stink gland would activate, and cause their breath to smell like a skunk for eight long years.

Yeah, Lolo was right, Randall had a temper alright, but get this will ya, he and Curtis became best friends, and many times, he would take Curtis riding on his back to show him what it's like to have wings. He did this he said because Curtis wasn't a threat or the cause of our extinction, he needed us to survive; unlike the humans who felt we need them for our survival.

Randall told me when I left that day after our journey with O. B. he had stayed behind with the ole wise one, and talked about the one who sits **higher than you can soar**. When he asked O. B. had anyone seen this person, O. B. answered yes – a human. Randall really got upset and said, "I just can't understand how a human could climb a mountain and see this person, yet we can't fly to reach him because he sits higher than we can soar." It just didn't make sense to him. Then he screamed, "Just look at'em Cindy! Look at'em flying like the sky belongs to them – flying like they are born with wings and meant to fly. They aren't Cindy; we are! Yet they fly – they fly farther and higher than you or I, so I'm told" And look, what's that horrible mist that comes from that airplane's tail feathers? It chokes the air we breathe and clouds our vision of a beautiful day. And they are superior to us Cindy? How is that so? O. B. said once this human laid eyes upon the one who sat upon high, he was bestowed a set of rules – rules that were supposed to be for the betterment of man and this earth. Well take a look around; they're doing a poor job of living by those rules. Huh! I'll tell you what's wrong.

He gave those rules to the wrong creation; he should've given them to us. I betcha he forgot all about us, or thought that we aren't worthy to fulfill those rules of order, Cindy. That's why I've got to go up there to talk to him, and tell him to put us in charge with those ah-h commandments. We would live by them and see that everyone else would, and maybe this place would be a better place."

He went on and on about what he was going to do and how, and I – well, I left him behind talking foolishly! I'd had all I could stand for that day. And poor Randall could've gone all night – no I take that back, in fact, that's what he did. When I awakened the next morning and gazed out into the meadow, I could barely see Randall still out there, perched in that same spot I left him in the day before.

From that day on, he was never the same and consequently, we were never the same. Oh sure, we were still friends, and when time permitted, we would still sneak off, just the two of us, as we had done before. But, there had been a time when I could stay around Randall all day and if possible all night, but after that day in the meadow I could only endure an hour or two. Everything would be fine until he started talking about his mission to seek out the one who sits on high – the one who sits **higher than you can soar**. And once he started on that, it would be every second, every minute, and every hour while you graced his presence – talking about reaching the mountain the human climbed to meet the Great One, Mt. Sinai; and talk to some burning bush I believe. And if it couldn't tell him where the Great One was, he would fly to the tip top and search there relentlessly, and then among clouds calling out this name O.B. told him that's been passed down by many before us, Father God of the Heavens and the Earth.

I must've heard this at least hundreds of times – hundreds of times too many. That's why I would make an early departure and leave him with his most admired, or better yet, loyal audience – the one who'd stay there and listen thousands of times if need be, Randall himself. And that's when I would spend most of my time with Curtis and LoLo – that is when she wasn't being old baldy's shadow.

12

Shoot, we'd find something to do even if it was nothing but take turns riding Curtis on our backs, now that his best friend didn't have time to do so. Ohhh, it really felt good being with my two friends, and leaving that mumbo – jumbo behind with Randall.

Anyway, the days passed quickly, as did the weeks and the months. Our youthful bodies now had transformed into adult ones, and all things we did as children were now put aside forever. Our days now consisted of talk of preparation for migration. And even though our bodies hadn't told us it's time to do so, our eyes spoke instead. We could see the meadow was no longer lusciously thick and green. Instead, it looked as though the sun had found its resting place. The trees looked naked and hungry; and at some point even frightened. The flowers refused to wake up. And animals, like squirrels and bears, were sporting their new winter coats – hardly taking time to talk to anyone, because gathering of food and its safe storage seemed more important at the moment. And the days – the days that once cast shadows long into the evening, now called them to bed much earlier.

We all knew what was happening, but then again, we didn't know. It was as it has been for the past three years; every animal and every plant's biological clock had alarmed, except ours.

"I feared this would happen again, but like each time in years previous, I remained optimistic – huh we all did – knowing a change would come. But again it looked as if our optimism was in vain." O. B. told us one day, as he, Randall and I were sitting there in the meadow, "I guess it's in the air we breathe, the water we drink, and the soil we walk on. You know, quite sometime ago all three were so pure you'd wonder how could this be. But over the years that purity has eroded, and perhaps that's the reason why you are in the state you're in."

"You know, it's a sad thing to see an animal one day and the next day he's nowhere to be found – he or his kind. It's like that wolf you told me about. I saw him early this morning lying there as

13

motionless as the stone he lay slumped against. I started to call out to make sure he was okay, but when I got closer, I saw his eyes were closed forever. Yet he donned a smile, so I didn't bother," he exclaimed. Then he rose from the ground and stood as tall as he could and stretched his wings as far as they could; commenting, "My coat is getting thick and yours is not. I hope your wings become fuller soon, because the slight chill in the air suggests that fall and winter is near, and you have a long journey ahead of you." He turned slowly and walked toward his roost saying, "I'm going to rest in that sycamore tree over there. I feel I haven't much time left, and neither does it."

Each day afterwards temperatures felt cooler than the days before, and the slight chill in the air suddenly became so cold it sliced through the flesh and clear to the bone. Fall had definitely set in, and somewhere in the not so far distant, winter would come roaring in. We were the only ones we felt nature had forgotten about. We were the only ones we felt were doomed to see another spring. But, one day about noon, I recall quite clearly while scrounging for food; something happened – something that I'll never forget for the rest of my life. A force from deep within emerged from the depths of my soul causing my entire body to shake violently, my eyes to move erratically, and my voice to sing out chirps I've never sung before. I suddenly knew which direction to travel, and being lost forever was no longer feared. I raced back home to tell the others the good news about my transformation, but when I reached home, they all knew. They too were going through what I had gone through – they too knew that it was time to go south.

With little time left, before the next day was to arrive with even colder temperatures forecasted – snow to be exact – we said our good-byes to all who were not in deep hibernation and left notes to those who had already succumb to deep slumber that read: "See you next spring." I was so grief stricken when I couldn't find Curtis to give him a hug, and LoLo struggled too as she and Bryan bid farewell until warmer days. Only if we had a few more minutes to properly say our goodbyes to those who were so dear to us, perhaps our tears wouldn't flow like a river, and our hearts wouldn't ache so,

both LoLo and I agreed. But at that moment the constant shouting of: "Let's go! Let's go!" reminded us there was no time for such sentiments.

So we quickly grouped together and took to flight in a V-formation – the young leading the old – with Randall at the helm as the cold northern wind constantly brushed against our tail feathers.

Faster and faster we flapped, never looking back as we did. Faster and faster we went, trying to make up for lost time as well. Through mountains high and valleys low, we journeyed. Through vacant fields and wooded fields, on we pressed. In no time, it seemed we'd covered many miles and neared our destination. The cold wind that trailed us both day and night no longer vowed the chase. Instead, a warmer, calmer wind now took its place.

Familiar settings were now being recognized by some of the elders who swore that our place of stay, our place of refuge, was just beyond the hills barely in sight. So, we decided to land and take one more rest before our journey's end. There in the marsh, we drank, we ate, but mostly we listened to the elders tell about how nice it was beyond those hills. Randall's parents were particularly most vocal. It seemed that their descriptions were most vivid. Perhaps this was so, because of all the memories theirs were the most intriguing. Their stories of good times past made some of us more eager to leave earlier than planned. But, the journey had taken its toll on many, particularly the old, so we waited – waited until the sweat which poured profusely ceased, waited until heavy breathing was restored to normalcy, waited until our weakness was overcome by strength.

But just when all agreed a few more minutes would do the trick and then our journey would resume – it happened! Loud crackling sounds came from all around. Birds! Birds! Birds all around us were falling down in pools of blood which leaked from their bodies.

"It's the hunters! It's the hunters!"

A cry went out. "Take to flight! Take to flight for your life!!"

Everyone screamed as all quickly took to flight. Yet, as we did, many were maliciously blown from the sky and their lifeless, helpless bodies plummeted to the ground. Randall's parents were among the unfortunate who didn't escape the bullets of the assassins. They and the others who were slain would never again see the joy beyond the hills which lay only a few miles ahead. It was nothing he or any of us could do but continue heading for the Promise Land. Perhaps there, we'll have the time to dry our weeping eyes and console our shattered hearts. That's all we could do!

Up, up and over to the place where basking in the sun meant everyday and all day long, and food remained plentiful all year round; and where crystal clear streams and enchanted waterfalls replenished and cleansed our parched weary souls. But when we got there something was wrong. The land which so many promised to be so much better was instead so much worse. The water was covered with this heavy thick substance which dispelled an odor of crude oil. Its shores were littered with broken glass, dirty syringes and paper as far as the eyes could see. The trees that were once vast now lay victim to man's expansion.

We didn't know what to do, whether to land, go, or stay. So we just hovered above, not knowing which direction to take. Our biological clocks, which served as a compass as well, had led us here and now it acted as if it had wound down, or even worse – broken. We were lost souls without a map and we knew we couldn't go back north. So we continued to hover in disarray – continued to hover until our exhausted wings couldn't hold our bodies in the air any more.

Every now and then, a bird was seen just falling from the sky from pure exhaustion, and no matter how we offered words of encouragement to stay in flight until we could figure something out, another would fall. It seemed in just a matter of time we all would succumb to the inevitable. But, just as we accepted what would be – would be, a call that was different from ours came echoing from the south. It got stronger and stronger as its carrier came closer. It was a flyer from a different flock that'd arrived weeks earlier. He said that everyday a member from a flock would fly up and warn latecomers the place they sought lay 50 miles further south.

This was salvation to our hearts, knowing that a Promise Land still exists. It brought joy to our souls and a resurgence of strength to our bodies that allowed us to toil on. So further south we proceeded under the direction of our new compass, our new clock – a flyer, whose call was different from ours, a flyer from a different flock.

In good time, we finally got there and sure enough the Promise Land many spoke of now lay beneath our wings; food, water, shelter, and a lighthouse standing firmly near coral reefs where the evening tide pounds them gently, embodied a ray of hope for lost souls. There, everyone was so happy and full of life, because there was no reason to be sad; everything we wanted was within reach of our wingtips. But Randall, well, didn't see it that way. He wouldn't smile for a second, even when one elder tried to offer some consoling words saying: "Perhaps your parents didn't make it because the Promise Land they spoke of so vividly didn't lie 50 miles further south nor was it 50 miles further north. Maybe it only existed in their hearts!"

He just kept to himself, perched in a grassy knoll by the stream, not allowing anyone to come near him, not even me. For a couple of days he was like this. Then, on the third day early that morning he arose and approached me. I knew what he was going to say, and I knew what he was going to do. So, I sealed his lips with a kiss and told him good-bye before he could utter a word.

Then he took to flight with the burden of the world on his wings, clouds in his eyes, and our love in his heart.

"I must go up there before there is nothing down here." He yelled out.

But before he was no longer visible, and no longer within the distance of my sobbing voice, I called out: "When will I know if you've made it, Randall? When are you coming back?"

"When the water is pure, the air is fresh, the soil is rich, and when man realizes his life determines ours, you'll know I've made it. Then I'll be coming back, Cindy. So keep watching – keep looking for changes. Then and only then, I'll be back!"

Wow! So many years gone by, and so many things happened within them. LoLo and old baldy are still together, and Curtis, well he finally earned his wings that following spring. O. B. found out that Curtis really was a rare species, one that takes nearly a year to cocoon and become a butterfly, and he's the slow one of the bunch – well the latter is what his family kidded about when they came back to get him.

"It's usually the special ones the Great Creator takes his time with to complete their cycle of life." O. B. fired back, giving Curtis something to smile about. "It is they who are given a special gift to make a big difference in the world." He whispered to Curtis as he bade him goodbye.

Oh-h, those days of despair and triumph, still warm my soul and cause my eyes to tear when looked back upon. But that's how it was – five years ago. It's hard to believe that the years have come and gone so quickly, and I'm still alive to witness that they have. My heart now belongs to another, and I've hatched three fledglings since, and all have begun to walk and fly. And even though it seems

as if all my time is dedicated to providing my family's every need, somehow I still find time to think of Randall.

Every time I see my little ones walk on clean shores, take a drink of crystal clear water, or take a breath of clean air, I see hope! I see change! Every time I see my little ones hover around humans as they throw pieces of bread in the air for them to feed, or see trees and flowers bloom with no fear, or we flock to the same place of winter's past. I see hope! I see change! I see Randall!